Original title:
The Garden Behind the House

Copyright © 2025 Creative Arts Management OÜ
All rights reserved.

Author: Harris Montgomery
ISBN HARDBACK: 978-1-80587-209-2
ISBN PAPERBACK: 978-1-80587-679-3

A Sanctuary of Green Dreams

In the corner, weeds confide,
A rabbit hops with silly pride.
Under the swing, my lunch gets caught,
By a sneaky squirrel who's quite distraught.

Tangled vines form a ticklish snare,
I dodge the spiders with quite a flair.
Butterflies chase the buzzing bees,
While I'm stuck just trying to sneeze!

Tales from the Secreted Grove

A gnome with glasses, lost his hat,
The turtles giggle, "Oh, imagine that!"
A ladybug plays peek-a-boo,
While the snails claim it's their best view.

Frogs throw parties in the warm sun,
They croak a tune, oh what a run!
But when I join, they leap in fright,
And I'm left dancing all night.

Where Wildflowers Dance

Daisies frolic, twirl around,
While dandelions play the clown.
The sunflowers wave like they're on cue,
And bees form a marching band, too!

In this patch, where laughter rings,
I trip on roots and lose my things.
Each bloom laughs as I tumble down,
In this flowery, funny crown!

Shadows of the Sunlit Glade

A gopher hides, thinks he's so slick,
But I see him dig—a funny trick!
The ferns gossip, swaying with glee,
As I attempt to climb a tree.

A game of tag with a sneaky cat,
Ends with me tangled—how about that?
And as the day fades to a close,
The flowers giggle, of joy, who knows?

In the Heart of Foliage

In the leafy lanes where jokes sprout,
A zebra in stripes, wandering about.
It laughs at the peas, so smug and round,
Claiming it's the king of this merry ground.

Lettuce plays hide and seek with the sun,
While carrots giggle—these roots have fun.
A snail sips tea, enjoying the view,
And all the flowers wear hats, it's true!

The Unfolding Silence

In this quiet nook, a frog sings low,
Donning a crown, it's the star of the show.
With a croak for a joke and a leap for a dance,
The daisies all chuckle, caught in their trance.

A gnome with a grin, he's lost in a book,
While shadows play tag with the moon's silver hook.
Oh, the antics of weeds, in their wildest spree,
Making mischief as they plot to be free!

Winged Champions of the Evening

Beetles in capes zoom past with great flair,
While dragonflies challenge the twilight air.
Two ants in a hurry, one drops its whole load,
They stop for a moment—oh, what a funny ode!

A firefly flickers, saying, "Look at me!"
While crickets debate who's the champion bee.
With laughter and cheers, the insects all cheer,
In the twilight's embrace, they dance without fear.

Palette of the Artisan's Hand

With colors a-splashing, the radish is bold,
It tells tales of summer and laughter of old.
The peas make a sculpture, all stacked in a row,
While the spinach debates how high it can grow.

An artist of fruit, sweet berries unite,
For a colorful picnic under the moonlight.
Each slice adds a giggle; each taste has its charm,
And the apples all wink, spicing up the farm!

Underneath the Elder Tree

Underneath the elder tree,
Squirrels argue, full of glee.
They think they're all the kings,
With acorns like shiny rings.

A rabbit hops by with a wink,
Pausing just a brief think.
"What's easier, a nut or a sprout?"
He chuckles loud, then darts about.

Where Wildflowers Keep Secrets

Where wildflowers bloom and sway,
Butterflies dance, no care in the fray.
They whisper tales to bees nearby,
Rumors of a fox who's rather shy.

Dandelions puff with pride,
Playing hide-and-seek, nowhere to hide.
"Guess who's the silliest flower in town?"
A thistle grins, wearing a frown.

Sunbeams and Shadows

Sunbeams tease the shadows long,
While ants march by in a happy throng.
One little ant lost his way,
Chasing a leaf that decided to sway.

A ladybug laughs, round and red,
While snails race while staying in bed.
"Oh, what a life!" pipes a cheeky crow,
"Too fast, too slow, who really knows?"

A Symphony of Bees and Blooms

A symphony of buzzing cheers,
The flowers sway, winking at peers.
A bumblebee conducts with flair,
"Watch out!" he barks, "A grasshopper's near!"

The petals blush at the lush display,
As daisies giggle the day away.
"Sing louder," one bloom does plea,
"Or I'll snooze away, just you wait and see!"

Rustling Leaves of Remembrance

In shades of green, a squirrel leaps,
While I sip tea and take small peeps.
The leaves gossip, rustling light,
As my cat plots a stealthy fright.

Memory lane on a grassy throne,
Where flowers blush and bees have flown.
Each step I take, a dance of glee,
In my mind's eye, pure jubilee!

The Sanctuary of Seasons

Spring brings blooms, I trip and fall,
The daisies giggle, I hear their call.
Summer's sun, I bake like bread,
With ice cream drips and laughter spread.

Autumn's crunch, the leaves confide,
As I dance on pumpkins, oh what a ride!
Winter's chill wraps up the fun,
Snowball fights, we're never done!

Cradled in Nature's Embrace

Once I found a tiny frog,
Wearing a crown made of a log.
He jumped and croaked, what a delight,
I laughed so hard, I lost my sight!

A butterfly made me her muse,
She chased me round, but I refused.
In this surround of glee and cheer,
Nature's laughter fills my ear!

Lanterns of Fireflies

At dusk, the lights begin to blink,
Tiny lanterns make me think.
Fireflies buzzing their bright show,
I catch one, but it says, 'No glow!'

The crickets join the night-time song,
As I trip over my own foot long.
In the glow of laughs and silly sights,
I dance with bugs until the night bites!

Nature's Quiet Confession

In the shade where weeds conspire,
A sunflower yawns, feeling dire.
The carrots gossip, thinking they're cool,
While brussels sprouts act like they're in school.

A squirrel steals lunch, what a cheeky thief,
Napping raccoons dream of a life without grief.
A crow caws loudly, crapping on plans,
While the daisies dance, ignoring the fans.

The Haven in the Wilderness

Tomatoes flirt in their red and green,
While a gopher digs holes, looking quite mean.
The old hose lies coiled, dreaming of glory,
As the ants form a line, like it's mandatory.

A butterfly winks, it knows it's a show,
While the flowers play peek-a-boo, putting on a glow.
Sunshine flickers, tickling the grass,
As the weeds laugh, saying, 'Just let us pass.'

Memory Lane Among the Flowers

Petunias recall their spring debut,
While daisies argue 'bout who's cuter, too.
A dandelion dreams of becoming a star,
But the roses roll eyes, 'We know who you are.'

The peas in their pod gossip all day,
As butterflies flutter, joining the fray.
A bumblebee stumbles, landing for a snack,
And the lilies just laugh, whispering, 'What a hack!'

Dancing Through the Green Maze

In the corner, a trowel rests, quite grand,
While the plants all mingle, taking a stand.
The mint leaves giggle, whispering sweet,
As the chives throw shade, thinking they're neat.

Hedgehogs roll dice, betting on snails,
While the marigolds cheer, recounting their tales.
A willow tree dances in breezy delight,
As crickets sing songs through the starry night.

The Lanterns of Dusk's Glow

Bobbing lights dance on the path,
Blinded bees start a laughing math.
Neighbors peek, noses pressed tight,
Raccoons decide it's party night.

A twerk-off between the beetles,
They groove to tunes from old stealthy needles.
Frogs in hats croak a silly cheer,
While fireflies giggle, full of warm beer.

The moon winks with a silver grin,
Lighting up all the chaos we're in.
Be careful, watch out, don't trip on a gnome,
He's just there planning his quirky home.

Thus life thrives in this zany space,
Where humor blooms with unwitting grace.
With every dusk, fun takes its chance,
And all of Nature joins in the dance.

Portraits of Nature's Edges

An old fence leans, asking for rest,
Paint peels away, it looks quite distressed.
But bees wear crowns, taking their strolls,
Painting flowers with honeyed shoals.

Squirrels wear socks that don't match at all,
Doing acrobatics, they dare not fall.
While rabbits gossip of their grand plans,
A carrot heist with hush-hush fans.

The trees pose in their leafy attire,
Whispering secrets, igniting desire.
Chickens debate who laid the best egg,
With roosters throwing in puns to beg.

Nature's edges dance with delight,
Each critter revels in their night.
Caught in the whimsy, we laugh and quirk,
In this odd gallery, we cherish the work.

Harvesting Silent Thoughts

Potatoes play peek-a-boo underground,
While carrots try to spin 'round and round.
Radishes hide with their blush in vain,
Sneaky vegetables causing us pain.

The pumpkins lounge, too big to hide,
Throwing a party like it's the Fourth of July.
Tomatoes gossip in shiny red coats,
Wishing to sail on tomato boats.

We gather thoughts like veggies in hand,
Collecting jokes from this whimsical land.
Broccolis flex their tiny green fists,
Saying they're better with cheese and mists.

Ah, the laughter that sprouts from the soil,
In the silent harvest, we revel and toil.
With each planted seed, a chuckle we sow,
In our playful patch, tender dreams grow.

Frosted Mornings and Sun-kissed Afternoons

Morning frost tickles the sleepy grass,
While freeze-dried laughs shuffle and pass.
Robins chirp shivers in woolly hats,
Huddling close with the giggling cats.

Sun-kissed afternoons beam with delight,
As shadows stretch taller, trying to take flight.
The dog jumps high, chasing his tail,
While some ants joke about one's big fail.

Daisies nod, sharing sunny puns,
Winking at clouds, while baking fun buns.
Sunflowers stand like silly guards,
Rolling their eyes at backyard regards.

With frosty mornings turning to gold,
The laughter echoes, never grows old.
In this merry cycle of heat and chill,
We find joy in each twist, each tumble, each thrill.

Imprints of Nature's Footprints

Beneath the swing, a spider weaves,
Her lunch bunch flies about the leaves.
In each cubbyhole, a squirrel hides,
While laughter echoes with joyful rides.

A hedgehog snorts, in muddy jest,
He thinks he's chic, in armor dressed.
The dog spins circles, chasing tails,
As laughter dances in the gales.

A worm pokes up, just to say hi,
A ladybug zooms, oh my, oh my!
With every stomp, the ants complain,
In this wild realm, they're uncontained.

A butterfly sports a vibrant tie,
While bees form bands and raucously fly.
Nature's circus, a funny sight,
Where every day feels just so right.

The Harvest Moon's Companion

The moon peeks out, a plump old cat,
Reflecting on where the veggies sat.
The pumpkins giggle, round and plump,
While carrots plot their little stump.

A scarecrow comes, his hat askew,
With birds that tease, they try to chew.
He protects the corn with silly flair,
One eye closed, as if he doesn't care.

A raccoon sneaks in for a cheeky bite,
While fireflies twinkle, oh what a sight!
"Eat more lettuce!" the veggies cry,
In this moonlit soup, they all comply.

Each thought unravels under the night,
As critters join in, with pure delight.
Nature's table laid out with glee,
For every beast, and bumblebee.

The Allure of Seasonal Whispers

Spring sneezes blooms, a floral sneeze,
As bees bring tunes with lovely keys.
Each petal giggles in the breeze,
While butterflies dance, oh yes, please!

Summer winks, the sun's a tease,
Popsicles drip down like warm cheese.
The flowers blush, oh such delight,
While kids find shade, in the warm light.

Autumn's here, with leaves that fall,
Squirrels plot, amidst their haul.
A pumpkin rolls, full of cheer,
"Let's scare the kids!" they shout, oh dear!

Winter whispers, "Let's bundle tight,"
Snowflakes giggle as they take flight.
In every shift, there's laughter pure,
Nature's whispers, a playful cure.

Crickets' Midnight Murmurs

In the darkness, crickets chirp loud,
Making music, their tiny crowd.
They tap dance on the moonlit grass,
While frogs croak jokes, oh what a pass!

A firefly blinks, a disco ball,
Spinning round, he almost falls.
"What's the buzz?" the night critters say,
As owls join in, in their witty play.

A raccoon steals a snack from the stash,
While raccoons scold him, "Hey, that's brash!"
But everyone knows, it's all in fun,
As laughter twirls with the setting sun.

So come join in this midnight spree,
When nature breathes, wild and free.
Each chirp and croak, a tune so bright,
In the fun of night, hearts take flight.

Fables of the Forgotten Bloom

In a patch where daisies dance,
And sunflowers wear a bright, bold pants.
The rabbits hold a grand debate,
On who can hop and not be late.

A bee with dreams of buffet time,
Wants nectar served with jingle rhyme.
While grasshoppers aim to sing,
But end up just doing the cha-cha swing.

The carrots gossip underground,
Of painted ladybugs they found.
When dusk arrives, they tell the tales,
Of mischief done with tiny snails.

So if you stroll through whirling hues,
With squirrels in hats and dancing shoes.
Just listen close, for laughter blooms,
In secrets held by hidden rooms.

The Whispering Willow

Beneath the willow's swaying arms,
The frogs play tunes with silly charms.
They argue over who's more slick,
While crickets chirp, their dance a trick.

A lizard dons a shiny cape,
Pretends he's much more grand than shape.
While whispers swirl with breezy glee,
Of flowers that paint the bumblebee.

The butterfly wore shoes too bright,
And slipped while showing off her flight.
With giggles shared among the bees,
As daisies chuckle with the trees.

So come and join the merry throng,
Where silly tales and laughter's strong.
In corners where the shadows play,
You'll find the fun that blooms all day.

Beneath the Garden's Skin

Underneath the leafy cap,
A snail makes plans for quite a nap.
He dreams of races, oh so grand,
While sipping dew in gummy land.

Mice with hats brew tea all night,
Debate the best way to take flight.
While worms conspire in secret lines,
To sneak some cake from roots divine.

A beetle boasts of shiny flair,
While spiders giggle, unaware.
Their webs will catch the dusk's delight,
As fireflies plan a disco night.

The slogan here is pure delight,
As critters twirl till morning light.
Each hour holds a silly grin,
For chaos dwells where fun begins.

Rhapsody in Green

In patches lush with painted fronds,
The toads are staging playful swonds.
With frogs in hats and boots so bright,
They leaped and twirled in pure delight.

A squirrel with a ukulele sings,
Of flying seeds and fluffy flings.
While ladybugs could clap along,
Their rhythm odd, yet never wrong.

The lettuces gossip in the breeze,
Of cunning raccoons and their thieving knees.
With laughter bubbling in the air,
As ginger cats play tag with flair.

So let the blooms hold vibrant tales,
Of funny tricks and comical gales.
Embrace the giggles, wild and free,
In nature's stage, just let it be.

Whispers of the Hidden Sanctuary

Among the weeds a picnic lies,
A sandwich tower reaches the skies.
The ants hold court at the crumb's base,
While bees debate the best honey place.

A frog with dreams of being a prince,
Wears a crown made of dandelion tints.
He croaks a tune, a grand serenade,
While rabbits dance in a wild parade.

With mud pies baked in the sun's warm glow,
Each splatter tells tales of fun in a row.
Squirrels chime in with a nutty jest,
As butterflies flutter, they're dressed for the fest.

A cat on the prowl thinks he's so sly,
With grass on his paws, and a determined eye.
Yet he trips on a stone, in a twist of fate,
And lands in a bush — what a silly state!

Secrets Among the Petals

In this patch blooms a jolly surprise,
The daisies gossip under sunny skies.
They whisper secrets of what they've seen,
Like the time that the cat wore a pickle green.

A snail with dreams of speed unmatched,
Challenges the worm who feels detached.
Yet the worm just laughs, slow and content,
As the snail hides under a leaf he bent.

The roses boast with their vibrant flair,
Claiming they've got the most luscious air.
But a raggedy tulip rolls its eyes,
And declares that humor is their best prize.

Butterflies flutter, they hold debates,
On who's the prettiest of garden mates.
But they all agree, as they twirl about,
That laughter here is what it's all about.

A Tapestry of Color and Shadow

In the twilight where shadows play,
A chicken struts, thinking it's ballet.
She fluffs her feathers, twirls round and round,
Claiming the title of queen of the ground.

A patch of weeds becomes a dance floor,
With rabbits tapping, they'd ask for an encore.
They hop and jiggle with nimble feet,
While crickets supply the rhythmic beat.

Sunflowers sway with a silly grin,
Challenging clouds to join in the spin.
But once the raindrops begin to fall,
They huddle together, one and all.

A lizard strikes poses like a true star,
As the fireflies join in, near and far.
Laughter erupts, from dusk till dawn,
In this colorful play, all worries are gone!

Blooms of Forgotten Tales

Beneath the old oak lies a tale untold,
Of a gnome who once thought he was bold.
He wore a hat made from mossy green,
And challenged the wind to a duel unseen.

Crickets gathered for a grand feast,
While ants debated who'd be the least.
With crumbs of cake and bits of pie,
They cheered for the gnome, who was passing by.

A scarecrow dances, feeling quite spry,
With crows rolling eyes from the fence nearby.
He thinks he's the hero, a legend in thread,
While mice hold auditions for roles in his head.

Yet as night falls on this whimsical place,
Stars twinkle down with a smiling face.
For in these blooms, laughter prevails,
With each forgotten tale weaving funny trails.

Whimsy of the Wandering Stream

A squirrel found a canoe,
He paddled with flair, what a show!
With acorns as snacks in a bag,
He's a river rat on a brag.

The fish rolled their eyes in dismay,
As he splashed about, took a spray.
'This stream's mine!' he chattered with glee,
While frogs croaked, 'Oh, let us be!'

Nuts were served at the side of the brook,
All critters came to see his hook.
Raccoons brought pies, what a feast,
And Mr. Duck quacked, 'I'll be pleased!'

So laughter flowed with the light of the moon,
While critters danced to a merry tune.
Who knew that a venture could go so far?
Next up, a raccoon auditioning for a star!

The Labyrinth of Sundrops

In a maze made of daisies and light,
A bumblebee buzzed with all of his might.
He lost track of time and his train of thought,
While chasing the shadows that sunlight brought.

'Oh dear,' he muttered, 'Where's my home?'
The wind gave a chuckle, 'You roam, little drone!'
He zigged and he zagged, through petals galore,
Till a ladybug yelled, 'Get off the floor!'

A chorus of giggles erupted that day,
As butterflies danced in a carefree ballet.
The bee found his way, yet decided to stay,
For the humor of flowers surely brightened his play.

And through all that chaos, the sun kissed the ground,
Beneath the wild laughter, new friendships abound.
So, honey was shared with mischievous grins,
In a show of silly love, the real fun begins!

Whispers of the Budding Year

The tulips wore hats, quite the sight,
While daisies donned shades—oh, what a delight!
A gopher was in charge of the show,
He juggled the buds, but they fell as they grow.

With petals a-flutter, the stage was set,
For a play about spring that no one would forget.
Critters all crowded for laughs and the cheer,
Just a critter or two with a side of sheer fear.

The sun cast its glow on the wondrous scene,
While ants formed a line, acting quite keen.
They'd waltz on a leaf, then slide on a flower,
It was the grandest of shows, gone wild with power!

So cheers filled the air as they flourished and spun,
In this jovial place, everyone had fun.
And as twilight fell, with a wink and a grin,
The earnest little blooms said, 'Let's do it again!'

The Creator's Green Palette

In strokes of green on a canvas untamed,
The brush of the gardener, swiftly proclaimed.
With each splash of color, a riot of glee,
The veggies had faces; come look and see!

A carrot curtsied to a cabbage so round,
While tomatoes played ball on the soft, loamy ground.
Zucchinis did jiggles, the squash sang a tune,
Oh, what a ruckus 'neath the glow of the moon!

With laughter erupting from each little sprout,
The kale joined the chaos, twirling about.
A spinach sought flight on the back of a bee,
While radishes laughed, 'It's our jubilee!'

So here in this haven, where nature's alive,
Creativity bloomed—watch the whimsy still thrive.
With every odd painting, a giggle would greet,
In the heart of the patch, life simply can't be beat!

Threads of Ivy and Time

Vines crawl like a lazy cat,
They stretch and yawn, just like that.
A squirrel argues with a bee,
Over who should claim the tree.

Old boots hang like forgotten dreams,
Recycling bins for hopes and schemes.
Weeds dance with the bumblebee pairs,
While gnomes freeze in awkward stares.

The swing creaks with each slight breeze,
Telling tales of summer tease.
A fort made of sticks and leaves,
Turns sticks to knights, oh what a reprieve!

Mismatched chairs narrate their regrets,
While the sun plays with no sunsets.
Days drift on, a funny disguise,
In a world where time quickly flies.

A Refuge of Stillness

A hammock sways with an absent mind,
Where secret thoughts are loosely twined.
A frog serenades the moon's own shine,
In a croaky voice, he claims what's mine.

The old cat watches the bugs go by,
With her one good eye and a sigh.
Grasshoppers leap, like jesters in flight,
While she contemplates her next big bite.

A birdhouse wobbles, nails on the brink,
It spills memories faster than ink.
Children's laughter fills the air,
As they try to climb trees without a care.

Chasing shadows is a silly game,
No one wins but we laugh all the same.
As fireflies blink in a giggly trance,
In this stillness, we find our chance.

Unseen Pollinators at Play

Bees buzz like tiny aircrafts above,
They drift and dive, they seem to love.
A butterfly flits with grand ballet,
Stealing nectar from blooms on display.

Ants march in lines, like miniature troops,
Carrying crumbs in their comical loops.
Their ambition's grand, though they're just a few,
Searching for a feast in the morning dew.

Hummingbirds zoom, oh what a show!
They play tag with the roses in tow.
A ladybug runs—wait, was that a race?
She pauses a moment, loses her place.

In this wild place, laughter is a sound,
Where flowers and friends blend all around.
With creatures unseen making mischief and noise,
Life's just a playground for all girls and boys.

Fragrant Paths of Solitude

The lilacs hum with fragrant cheer,
While gardeners try to keep it near.
A lot of weeds say, 'We belong too!'
A bunch of them laughs, 'Do you think we do?'

A rabbit hops by in a rush,
As if late for some big garden hush.
Laughter erupts from tulips in bloom,
As they gossip about that last snare tomb.

Sunflowers stretch up to catch a ray,
But the wind just teases them away.
A dandelion sends seeds like confetti,
While ants party hard, oh aren't they petty?

This place, a realm of giggles and sighs,
With each quirky plant, a new surprise.
In pockets of solace, silliness thrives,
In fragrant paths, where joy contrives.

The Hidden Oasis

In the corner, a gnome stands,
With a grin that's quite grand,
He whispers to flowers in bloom,
As if they were in a trance of doom.

Butterflies dance, a vibrant show,
While beetles plot in a secret row,
Who knew the weeds held such might?
They conspire in the soft moonlight.

A squirrel scolds a lazy cat,
Who dreams of catching a hapless rat,
The hedges giggle, the daisies chime,
As nature weaves a comical rhyme.

With watering can, a sprightly sprite,
Turns plants into hats, a silly sight,
The laughter spills as sun retreats,
In this patch where affection meets.

Nightfall Amongst the Vines

Underneath the grapevine's twist,
A ladybug makes quite a list,
"Dear ants, don't take my lunch today,
Or else I'll have to fly away!"

Moonlight glimmers on the leaves,
While a rabbit plots to steal some peas,
A chatty owl gives silly tips,
On sneaking snacks with nimble hips.

Crickets serenade the stars,
While fireflies mimic little cars,
Each breeze carries jokes of the night,
As shadows sway in the pale moonlight.

The garden comes alive with flair,
As creatures giggle without a care,
For in the calm of the darkened skies,
Mischief unfolds with laughter and sighs.

A Symphony of Rustling Leaves

The leaves are laughing, can you hear?
They're gossiping about the deer,
Who trampled the daisies in a dance,
Creating chaos while in a trance.

A raccoon dons a flower crown,
While chuckling at a snoozing owl's frown,
"Can't catch me, I'm the nighttime king!"
As the garden buzzes, joy takes wing.

A snail slides down a slick twig,
Thinking he's a superstar, real big,
But with a slip, he's off his course,
And slinks away with little remorse.

In rustling whispers, tales are spun,
Each creature's laughter a thread of fun,
As crickets chirp their goofy tune,
Inviting the joy of a merry moon.

Beneath Boughs of Memory

Beneath the branches, shadows play,
Recalling mishaps of yesterday,
A toadstool throne for a tiny king,
Says, "I'm busy; don't interrupt my bling!"

A sprightly mouse in socks so bright,
Dances about in pure delight,
Chasing after a sunbeam's edge,
With a leap that teeters on the ledge.

Old scarecrows crack jokes so sly,
As clouds drift lazily in the sky,
The garden holds stories, oh so grand,
Of laughter, shenanigans, and frolic in sand.

So come and sit, take a break,
Join the fun, for goodness' sake,
In this patch of lovable mess,
Where every moment is a playful guess.

Journey into the Wilderness Within

In the backyard, weeds have a spree,
Dancing like they're wild and free.
The gnomes keep a watch, so stout and wise,
While squirrels plot snacks, oh what a surprise!

With every shovel, new mysteries wake,
A plastic dinosaur hidden by a rake.
The flamingos giggle, leaning so shy,
As dandelions whisper, "We're just passing by!"

Behind the fence, there's chaos galore,
With rubber chickens clucking, oh what a chore!
Tomatoes wear sunglasses, strutting in style,
And carrots tell jokes, making me smile.

So enter this realm of botanical lore,
Where laughter is secret and weeds yell for more.
With every strange twist in this leafy tomb,
Life's utmost folly finds room to bloom!

Soliloquies of the Still Waters

A pond in the corner reflects cloudy thoughts,
With frogs giving speeches, they're quite a lot.
The fish roll their eyes at the chatter so loud,
While dragonflies hover, distinctly proud.

One duck, quite the philosopher, quacks about fate,
While others waddle past, in a hurry, can't wait.
The lilies engage in a silent debate,
Over which one's the fairest, oh what a state!

The sun spills its laughter, warms every face,
As turtles in sun hats move at a slow pace.
Reflections of nonsense ripple and gleam,
Where water jokes bubble up like a dream.

So here in this realm of the still and the spry,
Nature's own stage where oddities fly.
The whispers of waters and quacks intertwine,
Creating a comedy, endlessly divine!

The Rustle of Ancient Roots

Underneath the surface, the roots have a plot,
They gossip and giggle, and guess who's not?
The elderwood whispers secrets of old,
While mushrooms play poker, their stories retold.

A cart of lost socks lies found near the elm,
With rumors that fairies are running the realm.
The twigs keep a tally of all the lost shoes,
While ants file complaints on who gets to snooze.

The wind sings a tune, quite off-key, I fear,
But the ferns sway along, full of cheer and good cheer.
Crickets tap dance on acorns with pride,
As roots prattle tales of the things that they hide.

So linger and listen to laughter that flows,
With vines that weave humor in all that they pose.
In this tangled expanse of the ancient delight,
The rustle of laughter greets every night!

Evening's Gentle Kiss

As twilight arises, the fireflies take flight,
They're casting their glow in a novel delight.
The hedgehogs have gathered for stories and games,
While crickets compose opera using just names.

The sun bows out, but the moon's quite a tease,
With shadows that play tag, drifting with ease.
The cat ponders deeply, with plans to outsmart,
The raccoons with quarrels, oh whose is the tart?

A blanket of stars, like sprinkles on pie,
Winks at a squirrel who's asking just why.
The laughter of nature hangs soft in the air,
Where even the owls give a hoot without care.

So revel in moments, let worries all drift,
While evening's soft kiss is the sweetest gift.
In this quirky ballet of night's warm embrace,
Find humor and joy in each whimsical space!

The Silent Symphony of Growth

In the daytime, bugs all dance,
With ants holding a silly chance.
Worms in tuxedos dig right down,
While grass blades wear a leafy crown.

The tomatoes float like big red balloons,
While cucumbers hum cheerful tunes.
The daisies chat, while bees are shy,
As daisies giggle, oh my, oh my!

Berries hide in their fuzzy clothes,
Making faces at the garden's prose.
Rabbits hop, a comedic race,
With squirrels judge in a secret place.

When night falls, under the moon,
Crickets' lullabies are quite a tune.
And in the dark, with stars aglow,
Plants whisper secrets that we don't know.

Treasures of the Hidden Oasis

In a patch, a treasure lies,
With gnomes slipping on their ties.
Pumpkins giggle, a playful sight,
As frogs wear crowns and jump with delight.

Butterflies flutter, confused and lost,
Chasing each other at a silly cost.
Radishes wave with pointy hats,
Whilst snails slow dance with their scaly mats.

Spiders spin webs, a funky lace,
As young sprouts giggle, unfurling with grace.
And don't forget the wise old tree,
He tells tales of what used to be.

In laughter and joy, the sun plays peek,
Where each petal and leaf seems to squeak.
A riot of colors, a joke so bold,
The hidden joys of nature unfold.

Whispers of Blooming Dusk

As dusk falls, the flowers yawn,
And sleepy bugs retreat till dawn.
Sunflowers stretch, reaching for dreams,
While shadows play in evening beams.

Crickets start their nighttime cheer,
With fireflies twinkling, bright and near.
Mice bring snacks, a feast they hold,
With strawberry pie that's a sight to behold.

The herbs exchange their quirky puns,
As peas play hide and seek for fun.
A raccoon sneaks in with silly grace,
Making faces, a funny race.

And as the moon grins in the sky,
Each creature joins in without a sigh.
In whispered tales of growing love,
The night's a stage from stars above.

Secrets of the Hidden Haven

Tucked away, where the wild things play,
A squirrel finds acorns, his buffet.
Roses tease, with their prickly charms,
While petunias giggle in floral arms.

The path leads to mischief, oh so sweet,
With dandelions hiding, a bustling fleet.
Jellybeans grow from licorice roots,
Leading the scene to candy pursuits.

Lizards lounge with a flair so grand,
While tomatoes boast of their red band.
A sprinkling of laughter floats through the air,
As ants throw a party, without a care.

In this haven, secrets bloom anew,
With every leaf, a story or two.
A silly place where magic reigns,
And nature's quirks delight like trains.

Pathways of Tranquility

In the patch where weeds take flight,
A squirrel plans a daring heist.
With acorns neatly piled up high,
He dances like a tiny spy.

The gnome with paint chipped on his cheek,
Casts judgment on the birds that sneak.
They steal his hat, he shakes his fist,
But they just giggle, none have missed.

Sunflowers nod, with very tall grace,
As rabbits bounce with speedy pace.
One trips, does a somersault grand,
While butterflies cheer and clap their hands.

The blooms share tales of days gone by,
While beetles play but hardly fly.
Each flower's petal, a sleeve to wear,
As bees buzz jokes without a care.

Traces of Lost Journeys

A worm once took a trip too far,
And ended up beneath the car.
He waved goodbye with a slimy grin,
Now he's in traffic, what a spin!

The ants are marching, one by one,
To picnic grounds, oh, what fun!
But one gets lost, it's plain to see,
Now he's just sipping on sweet tea.

A toad sat planning his big leap,
Instead, he fell into a heap.
The crickets laughed, oh what a sight,
While beetles raved, "Let's dance all night!"

Each pebble's tale, a story spun,
Of who got lost and who had fun.
With chuckles echoing far and wide,
In nature's jest, we all take pride.

Serpentine Trails of Wild Onion

In fields where onions twist and twirl,
A snail decided to take a whirl.
He slid on greens and painted his shell,
Thinking he'd do it quite swell.

The fragrant herbs had much to say,
"Slow down, dear friend, and play our way!"
But he was racing with quite the flair,
Zipping past flowers, not a care.

A dandelion sneezed and blew,
Sending seeds in a playful crew.
The snail just laughed with all his might,
"Let's turn this stroll into a flight!"

As carrots giggled, roots all grinned,
"Join our parade, let the fun begin!"
With laughter snaking through the air,
Now everyone's tangled in carefree flair.

Harmonics of the Fluttering Wing

A parrot perched upon a branch,
Sings pop songs with a goofy stance.
While flowers sway to every beat,
And caterpillars tap their feet.

Bees join in with buzzing tunes,
As ladybugs dance under the moons.
The wind chimes jingle, a wild band,
With grasshoppers leading, oh so grand!

A butterfly flutters, posing just right,
"Look at me, I'm a bird tonight!"
While frogs croak solos with great flair,
"This music's magic, none can compare!"

The sun peeks in with a cheeky grin,
As nature's party spins and spins.
With laughter airborne, none can cling,
To the harmonics of each wing.

Underneath the Secret Canopy

The tomatoes rebel, they won't stay still,
They bounce and they roll, what a garden thrill!
Rabbits conspire with the gnomes at night,
Plotting a heist in the pale moonlight.

A squirrel in a suit, oh what a sight!
Debating with crows, a real feathered fright.
Who knew the radishes could be such a tease?
Dancing and prancing, they sway in the breeze.

One day I found bees in a funny old hat,
They claimed to be lawyers; I laughed at that!
Their buzz was a contract, a sweet little deal,
To protect the petals and negotiate zeal.

Under the sun, mischief does roam,
In this quirky patch, we all call home.
With laughter and sprouts, each moment does bloom,
In the shadiest nooks, hello, we consume!

Vestiges of Forgotten Visits

A lizard in shades, soaking up rays,
He tells wild stories of his glory days.
The daisies giggle, they sprout in delight,
As worms write ballads deep under the night.

The chair once belonged to a grumpy old man,
Now it's a throne for the insects' grand plan.
With crumbs on the surface it stands full of pride,
As ants hold a party, they won't let it slide.

Oh, what a sight! A frog wearing a cape,
He croaks like a bard, oh, what a landscape!
Unwanted guests in this wild affair,
The weeds show up dressed, no one's made aware.

Soft breezes carry their mischievous glee,
As the sun sets low, it's a sight to see.
Memories linger of visits long past,
Each moment relived, each laughter will last!

Tales from the Verdant Nook

In the shade of the lilacs, a cat takes a nap,
Dreaming of mice in a very neat map.
The flowers flirt wildly with bees flying through,
Whispering secrets of the garden's old crew.

One day a snail had a race with a worm,
Slow and steady with pals to confirm.
The daisies sang loud with a jazzy old tune,
While the daisies declared it 'A Day of the Moon!'

A hedgehog rolled by wearing nothing but spin,
Said he sought a crown for the garden he's in.
With a wink and a nudge, he called out for flair,
As the sun blushed pink, all the critters would cheer.

So laughter lived soft in this lively abode,
With each twist and turn on its quirky old road.
In this nook, so bright, stories twinkle like stars,
Under leafy umbrellas, they'll dance under Mars!

Where Moonlit Shadows Tread

At twilight, the shadows break into dance,
A raccoon in slippers just adds to the chance.
Fireflies dress up in their best little suits,
While owls host poetry, reciting their hoots.

The pumpkins plot mischief with giggles galore,
"Let's roll down the hill, we could win an encore!"
The corn stalk is laughing, it sways to the beat,
As the chill in the air gets swept off its feet.

Crickets keep time with a jazzy old song,
While petals sway gently, they hum along strong.
Each creature is merry in this verdant fest,
Celebrating the night where nature's a jest.

So come take a peek where the laughter is fed,
In shadows that twinkle, where fun folks have tread.
Each moment's a treasure, a joyous parade,
In the moonlight's embrace, all witticisms played!

Echoes in the Twilight Flora

In the dusk, gnomes start to dance,
Chasing fireflies, taking a chance,
A squirrel juggles acorns with flair,
While a rabbit snores in its lair.

Worms throw a party, oh what a sight!
With tiny hats, they groove through the night,
Bees bring the beats, buzzing in tune,
As crickets play the fiddle by the moon.

The hedgehog puts on a comical show,
Rolling around—it's a one-hedgehog show!
Flowers giggle in the gentle breeze,
Tickling each other with such great ease.

But watch your step, do tread with care,
For frogs declare it's their throne affair!
Jumping jests and silly little screams,
Welcome to night's delight, in our dreams.

Beneath the Arched Canopy

Beneath the leaves, secrets are spun,
Where ants march proudly like they've just won,
A beetle with shades, looking so cool,
Is strutting his stuff like he owns the school.

A snail's on strike, slow as a breeze,
With tiny picket signs, it's quite a tease,
While butterflies flutter with gossip and cheer,
Knitting their tales from flower to sphere.

The peacock prances, his feathers on show,
While doves gossip softly about the grass grow,
"Did you see that worm get tangled in twine?"
"Such a klutz, he's still trying to find his own line."

Lizards wear ties for a classy affair,
Inviting the ants for a feast, if they dare,
In this little world where the humor is found,
Laughter echoes, all around.

The Colorful Refuge

In the patch of daisies, giggles ignite,
As ladybugs giggle, oh what a sight,
A flower prances, its petals all bright,
Complaining that sun is not coming right.

A quirky old tree shares tales of the past,
Of all the wild critters that dashed by so fast,
"Last Tuesday, a cat tried to climb on my back!"
And everyone laughed as they viewed the attack.

With cucumbers on hats, the veggies parade,
While carrots do jazz hands, the funny charade,
"Look at us!" shouts a pompous old beet,
"Fresh and so vibrant, our style can't be beat!"

The sunflowers sway to the comical beat,
Dancing and joking, they're light on their feet,
As laughter sprinkles through petals anew,
This whimsical realm, where dreams come true.

Serenade of the Petal's Embrace

A bouquet of laughter fills the warm air,
As roses debate who has finer flair,
"Oh, look at me!" one flower will plead,
"Is there a greener stem? Tell me, do lead!"

Bumblebees buzz a ridiculous tune,
Singing to daisies, under the moon,
While tulips tap dance with whimsical feet,
Inviting each critter to join in the beat.

The sun sets low as the fireflies glow,
And frogs host a concert with a raucous show,
A patch of mischief, where humor does bloom,
In a world full of laughter, no room for gloom.

As night drapes his cloak, whispers take flight,
A chatter of critters that sparkles with light,
In this sweet serenade, fun knows no end,
In a petal's embrace, where all are a friend.

Companions of the Blooming Hour

In the midst of petals bright,
A gnome has lost his pointy hat.
The rabbit claims it's quite a sight,
As squirrels laugh and chat.

The daisies gossip with the breeze,
While bees buzz tunes of sweet delight.
A dance-off starts beneath the trees,
With worms in quite a fright.

A frog has stolen all the show,
Jumping high with leaps of flair.
The flowers cheer, "Oh, look at Joe!"
As butterflies float in the air.

Underneath the busy sun,
Each critter brings its own good cheer.
In this wild world, oh what fun!
Who needs a chair when you've got a deer?

Forest of Forgotten Secrets

In shadows deep, where whispers dwell,
A raccoon tells of pies in stew.
Yet every tale he spins so well,
Ends with a dance on muddy shoe.

The owls hoot in playful glee,
As ants parade on a mossy track.
"Who forgot to serve the tea?"
The hedgehog quips with a loud clack.

Beneath the ferns, the laughter flows,
While a turtle claims the crown of grass.
Each secret shared, like petals, grows,
Revealing that the time would pass.

In this woods of twisted thought,
Nature hosts a wacky ball.
With every squirrel, the merriment caught,
Secrets tumble down, one and all.

The Alchemy of Soil and Sky

The earth and sky mix like a brew,
As worms start mixing concrete plans.
A crow complains, "What's wrong with you?"
While planting seeds in towering cans.

The daisies wear hats made of rain,
While sunshine melts a cold debate.
The sunflowers wave, "We love the gain!"
As crickets dance to the feathered fate.

Here, every weed has dreams to grow,
With tangled roots in talks of spring.
A shout goes loud, "Now, look at Joe!"
As grasshoppers join in song and swing.

With laughter in the open air,
Each bloom's a jester, bright with cheer.
The moon takes notes, if he can bear,
And schedules laughs for every year.

Chronicles of the Dappled Path

On a winding road of green delight,
A cat declares it's time for tea.
With cupcakes baked by the morning light,
While frogs hop in jubilee.

The path is sprinkled with tales untold,
As mushrooms gather to conspire.
In a council where laughter's bold,
With a tree that plays the lyre.

"Hey there, pal, you've got a spot!
Your hat is bigger than your head!"
The hedgehog exclaims with such a plot,
As butterflies join the spread.

Each turn reveals a giggle's thread,
With stories woven in each flower.
Beneath the sky, so overhead,
The memories bloom with every hour.

The Secret Pathway to Bliss

In a tangle of weeds, the gnomes have a dance,
They twirl under leaves, in a whimsical trance.
A squirrel with a hat is the DJ tonight,
He spins woodchip records in the warm, starry light.

The flowers are giggling, they feel quite spry,
Bees buzz in disco moves, oh my!
A rabbit hops in, wearing glasses so round,
With every step he takes, he laughs at the sound.

The moon is a spotlight shining down on the show,
While shadows do the moonwalk, putting on a glow.
In this secret abode, where silliness reigns,
Laughter's the guest who forever remains.

So if you should wander, and hear merry cheer,
Join in the fun, there's nothing to fear.
The plants are quite jolly, not just green and still,
In this hidden realm, you'll find pure thrill!

Reflections in the Dew

Morning dew drops sit like jewels on a leaf,
A chubby worm gazes, lost in its grief.
"Oh why must I wriggle, and not frolic free?"
Sighed while admiring a bunny's grand spree.

The daisies are chuckling at the ants in a line,
Who march with their crumbs, thinking they're fine.
A ladybug giggles, then takes off in flight,
Chasing a butterfly dressed as a knight.

Reflections below show a world so absurd,
Where even the weeds have their stories heard.
A robin complains about fashion and style,
"That worm is out-dressing me," in denial all the while.

As the sun wakes the garden with a golden embrace,
Each creature is laughing, reveling in grace.
Join in the laughter, bring joy to the dew,
For the day's just beginning, and it's waiting for you!

Time's Resting Place

Among petals and grasses, time goes on a stroll,
Where old toads exchange tales, it's their favorite role.
"I caught a fly yesterday, it was quite a feat!"
Said one with a croak, as he settled for sleep.

A wise tortoise whispers, with stories galore,
About adventures and hiccups from yesteryear's score.
The sunflowers nod, sporting hats made of sun,
They gossip and chuckle, while shadows just shun.

"Tick tock," says a clock sitting high on a vine,
"Yet I'll never rush; there's no need to confine."
As time takes a nap in this whimsical space,
Nothing ever ages, it's a curious place.

So if you should wander and find time at rest,
Know that it's laughing, feeling quite blessed.
For here in this realm, humor is prime,
Each moment is playful, an eternity of rhyme.

Journeys Through the Foliage

Adventures abound in the leafy green maze,
Where snails take their time, reflecting their ways.
A fox in a cape darts out for a snack,
While mushrooms do yoga, there's no turning back.

Crickets are singing the night's favorite tune,
As fireflies dance under the big, silver moon.
A raccoon with a map leads a gathering crew,
"Let's find the best berries and have a grand stew!"

The path winds with laughter, the slippers of plants,
Whisking all travelers into curious chants.
A parrot makes puns that are so delightfully bad,
Its feathery friends giggle, "Oh, how we're glad!"

At dusk when the stars start twinkling in array,
Every leaf holds a secret, waiting to play.
So come join the journey, it's never too late,
In this forest of fun, you'll find your true fate!

Sanctuary of the Daydream Wanderers

In a patch of wildflowers, we lie,
Gazing at clouds in the sky.
A bee does a tango, buzzing with glee,
While ants throw a party, just you and me.

Dandelion wishes float with the breeze,
Tickling our noses, with such silly ease.
A squirrel steals snacks from our picnic spread,
Pretending it's clever, but we know its head.

The sun tickles our toes as we bask in the glow,
While crickets compose tunes that only we know.
In this quirky haven, laughter unfolds,
As we toss our dreams into sunbeams of gold.

With a hop and a skip, we dance in the weeds,
Chasing after shadows and whimsical deeds.
Time wobbles like jelly, as we play our part,
Creating a symphony straight from the heart.

The Quiet Symphony of Earth

A plump worm waltzes with grace underground,
In this puzzling ballet, no one makes a sound.
While squirrels critique from their lofty heights,
Debating which nut is the best for their bites.

The robin, a diva, sings off-key tunes,
While daisies giggle at starry-eyed moons.
The mud pies are fashion, a glamorous mess,
Yet each little creature feels utterly blessed.

Ants build their empires, quite proud of their feat,
As caterpillars dream of their transformation sweet.
While mushrooms hold council, a mystical crew,
Discussing the gossip of moths passing through.

Beneath willow whispers, the chaos finds peace,
Life's nonsensical rhythm brings laughter's release.
With every odd moment, tickling our minds,
We unearth the joy that true wonder finds.

Hidden Treasures Amongst the Foliage

In the thicket where secrets snicker and peek,
A frog wears a crown, or so it would speak.
Throwing ribbit parties, with gusto and flair,
Inviting all critters, and they all declare.

The hedgehog, a joker, rolls close to the vines,
Making the chickens break out into lines.
While beetles in bow ties negotiate peace,
Between ants and the roaches, for snacks they can lease.

The sunflowers gossip, their heads held up high,
Sharing the news of the moth passing by.
In a game of hide and seek, leaves brush our feet,
While laughter erupts from a wispy retreat.

When dusk throws a blanket in shades of delight,
Fireflies dance softly, igniting the night.
In this strange little world, where humor runs free,
Hidden treasures abound, just waiting to be.

A Canvas of Renewal

A splash of color, oh look what we've got,
The veggies debate who'll be grilled on the spot.
While seedlings toss confetti, all eager to grow,
With whispers of radishes sporting a show.

Grumpy old toadstools throw shade on the sun,
Claiming their kingdom, come join in the fun.
But the daisies are cheeky, and sway to the beat,
As bumblebees buzz on their soft, padded feet.

Sunlight dapples laughter over frolicsome ferns,
Where every small critter just waits for their turns.
A canvas of chaos, where whimsy takes flight,
Creativity blooming, all day and all night.

So come take a wander, a romp through the green,
In this magical realm, hilarity's the queen.
With giggles and wiggles, we cherish the day,
In the laughter of nature, we happily sway.

www.ingramcontent.com/pod-product-compliance
Lightning Source LLC
Chambersburg PA
CBHW062113280426
43661CB00086B/568